YOUTH HURTS

Youth Hurts

Sofia Maria Baja

2026

To my family,

To those trying to be found

Table of Contents

Merge

Let's merge our dreams
and never wake up
Sail away from the pain
that brought us together
And may we drift away
like a very soft feather
Whisper in my ear
Soothe and smooth
Spin me in the air
We've got nothing to
prove

I'll reminisce on the
late-night conversations
When the dim lights and
the music turn down
Left with the glow of the
night
While everything else
moves around
Darkness holds us tight
Anticipation trickles
through
Hesitation slips aside
Making me believe
anything can come true

Dreams

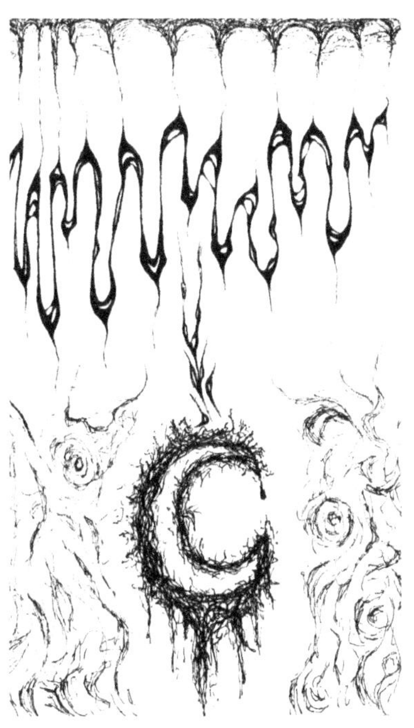

I think I'm afraid to fall
asleep
I'm not sure where I'll go
Who I'll see
Or how long it will be
I don't want to wander
too far
I'll start to drift away
I'm scared it'll linger for
the rest of the day

Only at Night

Only at night
I begin my fight
Pushing away the flight
One versus one
My eyes are shut
The dark creeps up
Like a monster from the sea
Why can't you just let me be?
I try to count
one
two
three
Let the thoughts be free
But they always come back
Ready to attack

Stuck

I need to find some
self-control
My life feels like I'm on
parole
Instead of being
proactive
I feel captive
So I'll self-medicate
When I should meditate
Or tear into my nails
until they bleed
And scroll endlessly on
my feed
All just to drown out the
reality of a life with
never-ending grief

It's supposed to come in
stages
But really, it just creates
cages

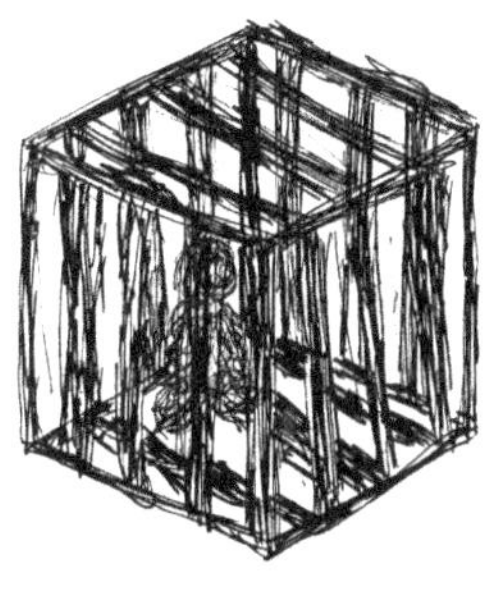

I'm behind bars with my
life on the other side
All I've done is cried
There are tear stains
embedded in my cheeks
I haven't showered in
what feels like weeks

Time isn't nearly relevant
Especially when there is
no present
Stuck in the before
Makes me sick to my core
I wish we had more
I can go on with a list
But what does it matter
when you don't even exist

Who am I if I don't miss someone?

Pounding headache
Swollen eyes
Swiveling lies
Spiraling the goodbyes

I've mixed love with pain for so long, I can't find the difference
I always yearn for those who hurt me the most because I loved them enough to let it happen
And I always want someone to cure me, even if they're the poison
So when I crawl into your skin
I resent the attachment I'm already in

I'm not allowing myself to leave our collected pile of past miseries
Just attached to the attachment
No answers for why

Now this abandoned land is where I lie
But I don't hate my life, I just hate what I'm doing with it,
and I hate how you toyed with it
Everybody told me to run
So I ran straight to you
Pretended your gun had no bullets
When you pierced them so gently into my heart

But it's time to realize closure comes from within, so
please don't come closer, even though I always pull you in

Fresh Grief

Feeling such fresh grief
Cutting it down, growing a new leaf
I don't want to go through this again
Please don't leave me, my only friend
I'm moving back
Starting over
In a city you never saw
As the girl you never knew at all

I feel the pain
I am the change
How did I lose so much energy at this age?

Moving so slow
Talking so low
I can't see straight
Or feel actual
Or actually feel

I'm blinded by my watery tears
'Cause I thought I'd know you for years

This isn't the way I wanted it to go
But oh, how it's going
And gone so far
Who blew the horn
And started the race
Too heavy trying to mourn
I can't keep up
I'm unfamiliar with this pace
I'll get there eventually
Just need to tie my shoelace

No Goodbye

I always go in blind
Someone stop me
So I can try to find some peace of mind
But how can I when it's so unkind
Feels like it's a curse
But maybe I'm just at my worst
Will you be here with me
Just to get high
Or will you leave without saying goodbye?
Do I have to beg for you to stay
I'll find another way
Just to have you for one more day

Ghost

I feel your touch as if it's a chill gifted from a ghost
Like a gust of wind gliding over my shoulder
Hovering over my skin
So close, my nerves grow colder
Did you feel what I felt?
Energy is never one-sided
You held my hand while we were never divided
But it always came down to what you decided
You're consuming my thoughts
Taking over every inch of my body
Because you can have it
Was it ever real?
Was it really there?
Did you know I'd break when you made the first tear?
I think I'll always wonder what's on your mind, so long as you continue to haunt mine
Now I'm left to daydream until you're no longer there to find

Savior

It started with a night
and shining armor
Who will pick me up
Wisp me away and find
my shiny shoe
I so badly wanted it to be
you
Will you be standing out
my window
Or rushing through my
door?
Oh, the bliss in ignorance
made from pure
innocence

So where is my savior? Is
it the boy in my bed
Are the answers in my
head
Hidden by the misty fog
of youth

It's ironic, because I push
everyone away, and the
ones I pull in always
never stay

I seem to be looking for
my savior in all the wrong
places
I've been looking for my
savior
In all the wrong faces
Someone please tell me to
turn around, look into the
mirror, 'cause all I need is
to scrub a little clearer

Addicted

I fall so hard
I never want to be caught
The rush of being in the air
Will always come down with a shattered landing
But it's a feeling that simply won't ever compare
It's naturally addicting
I struggle to know what's up or down
How did I get here?
Am I moving back or forward?
I can't tell
Maybe I'm floating in between
But we all know, that's never a thing

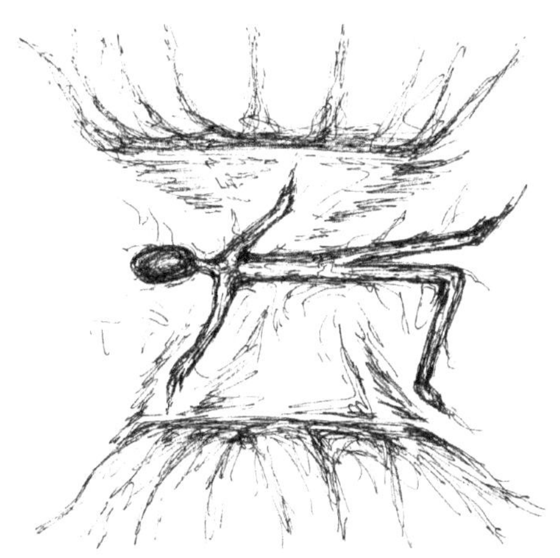

Damaged

There's always a push, then pull
No room for closure
Always left so unsure
Wait a couple days, then my arms are wide open
And you've already found something else to cope in

I know what you'll do next
I know what you think you can fix
'Cause we are one of the same
With different faces
And broken in different places
We keep thinking our scars are on the same side
But your left is my right
It's a mirrored sight
And all you still see is that we're both hurt
But your damage does damage
Even when your pull is tight
I hate that I'd still see you tonight

4th of July

Filled with the past
Full off our last
Fireworks fly
Just a fool in the sky
That's how I feel this July
Dazed with the bright lights taken down by the silence of the lonely nights
Hiding below
There are so many things you don't know
Yet you make me lose my mind
But that's one thing no one else can find

Love and Leave

Sometimes I wake up like this
Sometimes the middle of the day finds me like this
Sometimes the night wraps me up in this

And it may start with you
But it always ends with the realization of all my recurring relationships
That came so strong and left too fast

I can't get over the fact that people keep doing this to me
I know I said I was all or nothing
But you didn't have to give me your all and then leave me with nothing

I guess that's what the best ones do
They love and leave you like it's nothing new
Scream the words, wrap you in them, then wave goodbye
Maybe it's on me
I read the signs but didn't care to listen and follow
Whether they were good or bad
I was on a mission
Making my way closer to you
Not caring as I wallow

I miss you so much, I'm talking to you through my thoughts

Believing that you hear me too

Believing that you want to feel

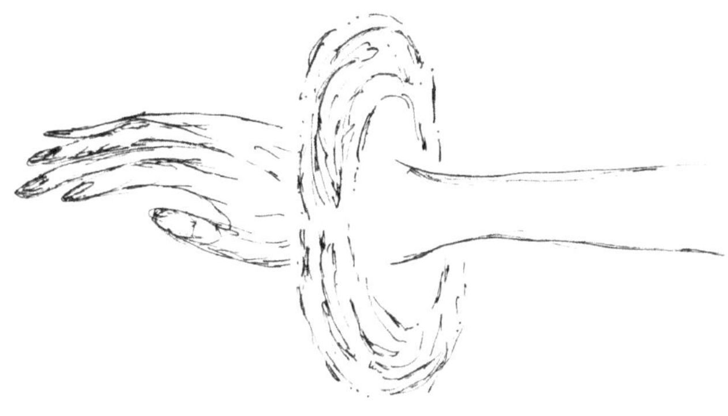

me all the way through

Sulk and Sonder

Sulk and sonder
Wondering in this ponder
Wandering no farther
I convinced myself that you cared
I thought because of everything we shared
Did you see yourself within me?
You knew I knew you
Is that why you ran away scared?
I'll stop questioning why once I start to get by

My head knows I should go
But my heart keeps saying no

So for now I'm here,
Craving the mistake that is you
Attached to the ache that grows within me
'Cause it's the grief of all that could be

Your Choice, My Test

Oh my!
Here comes another revelation
I have to say with some frustration
I keep forgetting how it felt
'Cause I feel nothing when I'm not on something
Not even when your dense memories hold so much weight
But you chose your own fate

So now I tell myself it's a part of some test
Trying to make me my best
Since your name feels like a bullet through no vest
Oh look!
You just created a hole in my chest
And I'll still call myself blessed while feeling possessed
From all these feelings I have so repressed

My soul will soon rest
But my head will always be in distress
And my heart will mourn its final test

Letting Go

I refuse to spend another winter crying over you
Saying goodbye makes my heart tear
But letting you go is a breath of fresh air
So for now, I'll see your smile in my head
And hold the ghost of you in my bed
I ran into your arms in hopes of swimming to the top
But instead, we drowned together tied like a knot

My Fault

Screaming with my lips sewn together as if I didn't pick
out the needle and thread
My body paralyzed, and my mind trying to catch up
Searching for empty love to ease the pain
It's stabbing me from every angle
Creeping behind my thoughts
Crawling me into a corner
Drowning myself in my tears of regret and sorrow
Why did you do this to me? I say looking in the mirror
It's just me, it's only me
And that's the problem

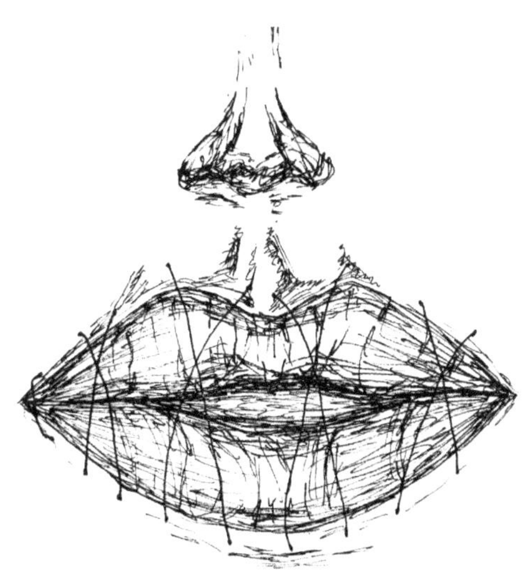

Head Infection

I get so discouraged
Looking around for some courage
I want to feel better
But I can't be a go-getter
Crying instead of trying
I don't want to fail, so I just bail
But fuck it, maybe it's all just a spectrum
I think I need some protection
Got to look at everything from a different direction
Discover some kind of self-reflection
From whatever you call this head infection

Yes, I know

I'm going through nothing if I compare
So I'm going through everything in despair
Saying life isn't fair
Because I care too much
Extremely sensitive to the touch

My brain is going insane over nothing
Breaking down even though it's not a something
I feel so foolish and naive
So I'll constantly get up and leave
I don't even say goodbye
Yes, I know that I'm the bad guy
I guess I'll just go float up to the sky

So Sober

I either feel everything at once or nothing at all for months
Trapped inside my head
Nowhere to fall
Sinking into the bed
What is this underlying dread?

The Mirror

January blues
Longing for a muse
Doing everything and nothing to not light the fuse
Crust falling from my skin
There are disgusts crawling from within
I'm hearing voices from the mirror
Insecurities are getting clearer

Can't find any self-esteem
How can I do anything?
All I want to do is scream
Never-ending comparing
Wild thoughts can't stop oversharing

Floating like a ghost
Wondering aimlessly
Rolling around restlessly
Constantly listing out my many options of things I'm not going to do
Because I'd much rather be with you

Some days are filled with gloom
And I can't find the courage to change the cloud above me
I'm drenched in rains of uncertainty

Feeling the doom of my own doing
Crying over things I can change
Crying over change, I'm not changing
Looking out at lives being lived
Looking at mine, only seeing from within

People of the Past

The numbers go down
I'm saying goodbye to the people of the past
It was great even when it didn't last
Now I'm watching their lives through screens
Living the worst of my teens
They'll never understand
So the jealousy sparks matches in my hand
Lighting fires throughout my body
Trapped with nowhere to go
So my words are the door, as you know
None of this is for show, even though I feel like a joke on stage
Sometimes in a cage
Grasping bars of rage
But it's okay, you're not to blame
I'm the one who carries the shame
I know we lost our connection
So I lost my direction
Can't look back now, too bad I resent my reflection

Pain is Pain

I should probably stop complaining about problems that I
cause
Wish I could call it a day
Unwind the roll
And wrap them up in gauze
Let it scab over
Make time heal all wounds
But I pick, bite, and scratch
Peel the layer that just grew
Place another patch
Pain is pain, never all that new

Lost in Decision

The classroom has killed
My only passion, my only thrill
Goosebumps on my arm
The thought of change
Always brings me a chill
It's my mindset
My cling to a safety net
Can't make a decision
Can't magically forget all that I regret
Weighing down my options
Anchoring my feelings
Lost in all directions
As I stare at the fan on my ceiling
Envying those with connections

I Don't Know

There's a burden of highs and lows
Constant answer of I don't knows
Fearing faces of fawns and foes
I'm running away
Is this really how it goes?

Holiday Fear

Christmas lights in the
kitchen
No one's trying to listen
Foggy days
Falling back into those
ways
I can't get off the floor
I'm longing deep down to
my core
Do I keep isolating?
It doesn't feel so good
anymore

I'm stuck in this
December
Wishing for a spark to
remember

Happy holidays for some
I couldn't be more numb

Waking up incapable of
trying
My body shutting down,
starting to feel like I'm
dying
Looking at the calendar,
constantly sighing

Can't find anything to
watch
Infinity of thoughts
cascading down my head
to my shaky feet
Won't listen to new
music
Nothings amusing

Hard to get out of
snoozing
Night drives, avoiding
the tides
Since it's that time of
year again
Preparing for the family
blend
Can't wait for the
amends!
I drink for holiday cheer,
but all I gulp down is
holiday fear

So let's just hope for next
year?

Patterns, Circles, and Shapes

I've been like this my
entire life
I can map out the
timeline
Run my finger across the
red string
Stand still in my orb
Say your name until it
doesn't sting
Watch as they surround
Listen to your voice until
my ears ring
Mark the highs and lows
on a graph
Fall behind, watch
everyone listen and laugh
Is this circle really my
only path?

I think in spirals
Drive around the block
Take another loop
Always end up in my
familiar route

I talk in patterns
Make the same lines
draw the same designs
Splash water on my face
Rinse and repeat
Choose the same flavor
'Cause I like the taste

I live in my cycles
Rooted in agony
Over and over, again and
again
Running up a wheel
My legs are aching

Trying to move while I
feel
Some days I'm too raw
Almost ill

But it goes round and
round
'Cause change keeps
changing
So why do I continue to
stand so still

Spare Time

We spare time, but time doesn't spare us
We block out time in our days
Change the schedule, change our ways
Find freedom in frolic
Paint the sky
It's a Wednesday, why not get high
Walk to the park, choose a flower to pick
Or grab a lollipop to lick
'Cause we live in our spare time

I'll tell you how I feel, but not what I think
Soften the blow
Anything can change in a blink
So I'll spare your feelings to spare my guilt
But time doesn't spare us at all
It rarely creeps or lurks
I wait outside its door, thinking that works
Time will jump and shout
Grab your shoulders, catch your breath
Speak your thoughts, make it count
Time isn't a number or a day
It holds the memories that fade away
It isn't a curse

Or a kind of fate

It chooses when to make us wait

So spare every fall

Savor what is

Before time comes for us all

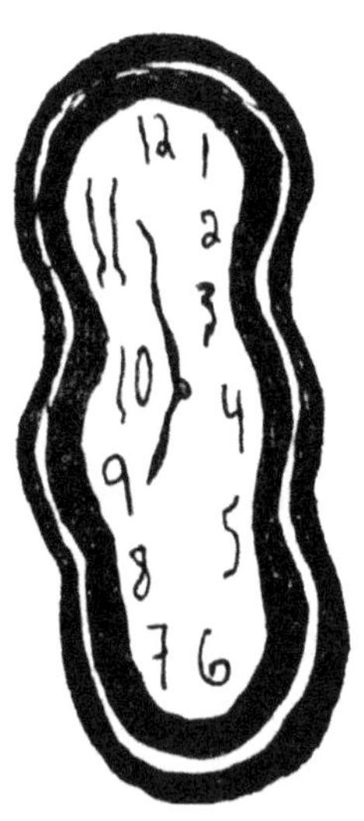

Staring at the Ceiling

The day is still, and the sun is warm, but I'm frozen in this room
My limbs are weak, the lights are low
My arms hang down to the ground
Barley moving, minimal feeling
Everything seems so slow
As if you're trapped in a dream and can't move
I can't grab out and reach
I'm stuck and all I hear is the clock tick
I lie and stare at the ceiling
Minutes and hours pass by so quick
I can't break free
Bound to four walls
Looking around, I know there's no key
Nesting in sheets, pillows, and dirty laundry
Roots grow, leaves fall, branches break, I am the tree that I make
My body tingles, and my chest is heavy

Embodying numbness through and through
I've gotta get out of my mind
And this room too

Bathroom Floor

I didn't want to be here
Somehow always in fear
Feeling like I need to shed a tear
While sitting on the bathroom floor
Always wanting more
Embarrassed of who I am
Headache from all that I can
How can I be back where I began?

Growing Up

I grew up breaking down
Why am I surprised I'm
still underground
Crying outside my
parents' door

Never knew what for
It was always inside of
me
Took over everything I
was going to be
Well, I found my own way
Stronger than everyone
else from the pain that
ruined me every day
While you were all out
just to play

They built castles in the
sand
While I talked to a
woman with a notebook
in her hand
Played dress up like I was
walking down the aisle
Now I'm constantly
faking a smile

When I was a child
I dreamed of getting
older
Maturing didn't come
with age
It forced its hand on my
shoulder

I learned grief at 10
So I was automatically
kicked out of the playpen
Feeling taller than my
peers
But brought down by my
tears
Developed irrational
fears
Up and down throughout
the years

Learned what life was
like at 16
It's normal never to feel
seen
Never happy or sad, but
always in between
Overcoming trials to be
put down under new piles
Lessons learned along
every way
Must lead to peaceful
acceptance one day

Grand Life

I may not live a grand life
With people to call
And places to go
But I have passion, and I have question
I feel beyond and don't need answers
I care so deeply that I am drenched
I am fooled into believing love is pain
I think happiness is temporary
I bleed for art
I cry for the past
I know my value even when it's hidden
I will not be taken down by grief
Whether it's mine or yours

Hello Moon

Whispering hello to the
moon
Listening to the sounds
of the rain
Letting all voices restrain
My body feeling tame
There's no more
flickering flame

I look up at the moon
Thinking of you
I look for truth in
questions
I stare at the sky
Searching for lessons

In unusual peace
In constant uncertainty
I gaze out my window
Pretending I landed in
limbo

Fresh air through my hair
All over my skin
Letting it through
everywhere
Make it wipe away the
mood I'm in

Covered in remembrance
'Cause I've thought of
you ever since
Now I shout hello to the
sun
Let it drench me

Drown my mind with
light
Forget all about its
battling fight

Watch the bees in the
grass
People watch until they
pass
Submerge in time until
the control is mine
I'm never stuck from it,
just still in it, with
purpose to be present
After all, this life is a gift
from the sky
Whether opened or not, it
will come by, and it's your
choice to fly

The Art I See All Around

I want to draw everything I see
And I want my drawings to forever be
Have the pen just flow
And may the brush just go
Please express every thought, feeling, and ache
So when I leave it
It's yours to take

Beach Day

Drawing in the sand
As you're watching my hand
Looking up at the clouds
Pointing at the spaces in between
Your blue eyes speak unspoken thoughts
Wiping my many blues away
Wish we could read each other's minds all day

Lying in the Leaves

There's children running around screaming
A man sitting in the corner
Wonder what he's reading?
Between the shadows and the light
Strangers are meeting
Casual conversation
While I'm staring in contemplation
I can sulk and sulk until I cry
But the trees stand still
The birds fly by
Realizing this is just a moment
For me and the man walking alone
For the dog chasing its bone
This too shall pass
When want turns to will
Nothing seems so fast

Maze

What if the idea is to get lost?
Never find a way back
Question every step forward
Be confident in guessing
Feel scared in the unfamiliar
Face anxiety with clarity
Find excitement in searching

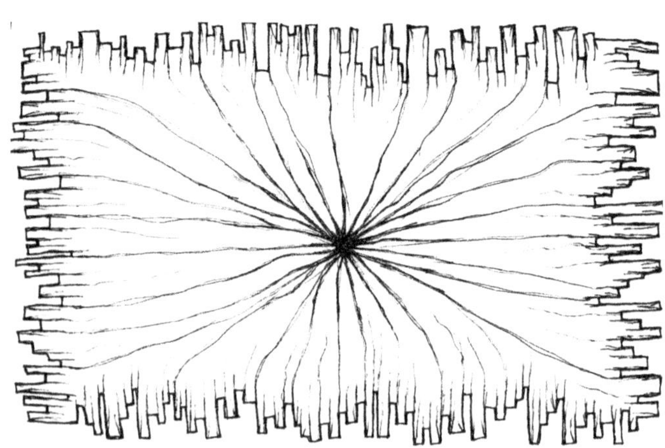

The Meaning

Standing on my tallest of toes
Not for a hug
Or a kiss
But for a reason in this bliss
I'm not trying to wipe away the mist
But you are just something I miss

Reaching for the visual I had in my mind
Or maybe it's a memory of some kind?
I tend not to know much of anything and find defeat in questioning
When that shouldn't be so unsettling
The answers don't exist, and the meaning is in the ability to feel
Even if I constantly resist the emotions that seem to be too real
It's like I'm scared of what I might actually feel
But maybe that's the only way to heal

www.ingramcontent.com/pod-product-compliance
Lightning Source LLC
LaVergne TN
LVHW011052110826
845149LV00015B/3474